HOW TO WRITE, RECITE, AND DELIGHT IN ALL KINDS OF POETRY

Joy N. Hulme and Donna W. Guthrie

THE MILLBROOK PRESS
Brookfield, Connecticut

IN LOVING MEMORY OF MY MOTHER,
WHO NAMED ME AND TAUGHT ME JOY.
J. N. H.

IN MEMORY OF JEAN CIAVONNE,
A FINE POET AND A WONDERFUL FRIEND.
D. W. G.

Photographs courtesy of The Metropolitan Museum of Art, Bequest of William Church Osborn, 1951. Copyright © 1991 by The Metropolitan Museum of Art: p. 8; Art Resource, New York: pp. 12, 14 (Tate Gallery), 19 (Erich Lessing), 27 (Erich Lessing), 55 (National Museum of American Art), 69 (Giraudon); Rita Baragona: p. 16; Desi Lustig (photo courtesy John Goodrich, Sirovich Art Gallery): p. 21; Joyce Goldstein: p. 39; National Gallery of Art: p. 48; Flavia Bacarella: p. 51; Su-Li Hung: pp. 73, 85; Norton Simon Foundation, Pasadena: p. 78; Marion Lerner Levine: p. 90

Library of Congress Cataloging-in-Publication Data
Hulme, Joy N.
How to write, recite, and delight in all kinds of poetry /
by Joy Hulme and Donna Guthrie.
p.   cm.
Summary: Young people are encouraged to experiment with a variety of poetic forms and to recite and preserve their creations.
ISBN 1-56294-576-9 (lib. bdg.)
1. Children's poetry—Authorship—Juvenile literature.
2. Recitations. [1. Poetry—Authorship.] I. Guthrie, Donna. II. Title.
PN1085.H45   1996
808.06'81—dc20   95-12607   CIP   AC

HOW TO WRITE, RECITE, AND DELIGHT IN ALL KINDS OF POETRY

CONTENTS

I N T R O D U C T I O N

In this book, you will find more than seventy poems written by kids just like you. Some of the poems are illustrated with paintings that were made by artists from long ago or from the present day. The paintings and the poems express similar feelings and ideas, but in different ways. Under each painting, you will find the title of the painting, the year it was painted, and the name of the artist who made it. After each poem, you will find the name and age of the poet. If the poet is not identified, the poem was written by one or both of the authors of this book.

As you read all of these poems, many different pictures and sounds will come to mind. That is the magic of poetry.

> Words can dance and dive and dip,
> Flitter, flutter, fly and flip.
> Words can jostle, jar or jolt,
> Comfort, calm, console, support.
> Words can nudge or bump or bang
> Jingle, jangle, chime or clang . . .
> It's up to you
> What words will do.
>
> When assonance and imagery,
> Heart-throb rhythms, lilting, free,
> Waltzing words and sounds that sing
> Combine in lines with rhythms that ring,
> They'll start a tickle, tingle, thrill,
> A climbing-up-your-backbone chill . . .
> You will delight
> In what your write.

JOY N. HULME AND DONNA W. GUTHRIE

The Manneporte (Etretat), 1883, by Claude Monet.

CHAPTER ONE
. . . .
WHAT IS POETRY?

The sighing sea, birds on the wing,
Thoughts sprouting out like buds in spring,
One sudden, bright, breathtaking sight
That fills your heart with sweet delight,
A tangy taste, a savory smell,
A velvet touch, a pealing bell,
A tender feeling. . . . All may be
A start, a part of poetry.

Poetry is a way of expressing deep thoughts or strong feelings using rich and beautiful language. Poetry looks, sounds, and feels different from other kinds of writing. It has a special appeal to your heart as well as to your mind. It often makes a complicated idea clear and concise. It is pleasant to hear as well as to say.

This book will introduce you to some of the tools you can use to make words waltz and sounds sing. Much of the poetry used as examples was written by children just like you and always includes the author's name and grade. If the author is not identified, the poem was written by one or both of the authors of this book.

WHEN DID POETRY BEGIN?

People were composing poetry even before history was recorded. Children learned the myths, legends, and beliefs of their people from their elders. Tales were told from memory. Often they were repeated in poetry or song. This made the stories easier for people to remember.

Poems were also praises or pleas to the gods and a part of religious ceremonies. Poems were sung while people danced. They were used like magical chants, perhaps to ask for rain for plentiful crops or for good hunting, or as part of healing rituals. Sometimes poems explained the puzzling events that occur in nature.

Even today, poetry is all around you. You can find it in books, in songs, and in the rhythms and sounds of everyday life. Sample it. Savor it. Collect your favorite lines, verses, and poems. Enjoy them again and again and again. Delight in the way they make you feel.

POETRY IN YOUR LIFE

Poetry has always been a part of your life. Your parents probably sang to you, read to you, and played with you using different kinds of poetry. You probably heard Mother Goose rhymes and fairy-tale chants even before you could talk. Your picture books were filled with poetic language. And did you ever twirl a rope to a jump-rope jingle?

> Teddy bear, teddy bear, turn around,
> Teddy bear, teddy bear, touch the ground;
>
> Teddy bear, teddy bear, read the news,
> Teddy bear, teddy bear, shine your shoes;

Teddy bear, teddy bear, go upstairs,
Teddy bear, teddy bear, say your prayers;

Teddy bear, teddy bear, turn out the light,
Teddy bear, teddy bear, say "goodnight!"

Do you remember choosing who would be "It" with a counting rhyme?

Eeney, meeny, miny mo,
Catch a tiger by the toe
If he hollers let him go
Eeney, meeny, miny mo.

All of these are poems.

WHY WRITE POETRY?

There are four main reasons to put your thoughts in poetry. The first is to express feelings or imaginings.

THE BRAVE RABBIT

Soft and furry,
White as snow . . .
Running scared,
trying to escape the hungry wolf.
He jumps into his hole,
His heart pounding . . .
Safe at last.

—*Alisia Sanchez, grade 4*

Sudden Shower on Ohashi Bridge, 1857, by Hiroshige.

The second reason to write a poem is to tell a story.

THE SOFT DRINK

As I raised the soda can off the shelf
I realized it was freezing and released it quickly.
When it struck the ground, brown liquid surged, with a
   thunderous roar, on to the spotless floor.
The hairy dog came and stuck out his big, red tongue.
I commanded the pet to get far away.
He sat down.
He stood up.
He shook off the brown liquid.
The liquid sprayed quickly off the dog's sleek, black hair.
The droplets that fell on my tongue were as warm as the
   dog's protecting fur. . . .

—Clay McKell, grade 4

The third reason is to describe a person, place, or thing.

SUDDEN STORM

The rain comes in sheets,
Sweeping the streets.
Here, here, and here
Umbrellas open
Red, blue, yellow, green.
They tilt and they lean
Like mushrooms, like flowers
That grow in the showers.

—Irma Quijada, grade 4

The fourth reason is to teach a lesson.

The cat stalks
teasing and resisting the temptation
of attacking too soon.
Finally, the moment comes—
He pounces down!
After devouring his prey,
he leaves
quickly, silently
with no remorse.
This is what he must do to survive.

—*Scarlett Kellum, grade 6*

Cat and Mouse, 1967, by James Lloyd.

CHAPTER TWO

THE TOOLS OF THE POET

Artists create with brushes and paint;
Sculptors use chisel and stone;
Potters mold clay with fingers and thumbs,
And poets have tools of their own.

Poets paint pictures, carve characters, and mold moods with words. The words you select and the way you combine them with others give your poetry its special meanings and effects.

Choose the words that contribute the most to the message you have in mind. Be specific. Say exactly what you mean. For instance, if you are describing the wind, think carefully about what it is like. Is it a breeze or a blast? A gust or a gale? A tempest or a tornado? What sound does it make?

The wind whistles through cracks at Yosemite.

—*Sara Prouty, grade 4*

A tree might be an ash or an oak, a birch or a beech, a sassafras, or a eucalyptus. There are also many kinds of flowers, each with a distinctive shape, color, or fragrance. Certain varieties bloom in

Garden Rhythms between Yellow & Blue, 1994, by Rita Baragona.

each growing season. When writing a poem, choose exactly the word that describes the picture you have in mind. Use a dictionary to clarify definitions. A thesaurus or synonym finder can also add to your word choices.

This poet described the flowers that were blooming in her spring garden:

A GARDENER TO HER GARDEN

I dress you up in daffodils,
Acacia lace, azalea frills.
A purple pansy petticoat,
A velvet violet redingote.

I cannot match your elegance
Dressed in baggy, mud-stained pants.

It is sometimes fun to invent your own words. Two words can be combined to form a new one. For instance, you could call a disastrous catastrophe a "disastrophe." You could say an activity that is wonderful fun is "funderful."

The need to make words in your poem rhyme may inspire you to create a new word. The meaning must make sense, however, or it will distract the reader from the rest of your poem.

An ocelot is like a panther.
What an ocelot is I cannot anther.

Behold the hippopotamus
From her top down to her bottamus.

—Zach Lorenz, grade 3

If your fingers fumble on the keyboard, you might omit a letter or hit the wrong one and accidentally discover a new and descriptive word that you can use in your poem: happimess, slopsided, godness, fightful, kictim.

 ## RHYTHM

Rhythm is the pulse of a poem. Like the throb of a heartbeat, rhythm is the regular pattern of sound in music and in language.

Poems repeat a regular beat
Like tappity toes and marching feet.
Like metronomes with tick-tock hands
Or beating drums, parading bands.

Words arranged in a pleasing pattern will ring in the mind like the lyrics of a song. Listen for the beat that repeats. If necessary, tap out the time with your fingers or toes. A good rhythm will make a poem easy to remember.

This cheer has a strong rhythm made up of short, quick beats.

One, two, three, four!
Who are we for?
Five, six, seven, eight!
Who do we appreciate?
Team! Team! Team!

Can you hear the rhythm of this poem? Each line has either three or four beats.

MARCH

When winter weather's on the wane
And spring has not yet sprung,
March swaggers through the calendar
Just sticking out his tongue
And daring you to speculate
Which way he'll choose to go.
When crocus pokes a purple nose,
He'll cover it with snow,
Then send the sun to warm the ground
To make the tulips grow.

Street in Paris, Rain, 1877, by Gustave Caillebotte.

He'll whip up wind; he'll sling out sleet;
He'll puddle mud around your feet.
And when he's broken every rule,
He'll turn the page to April Fool.

 TEMPO

Tempo is the rate of speed at which the poem moves. The content and feeling of the poem should determine the tempo. For instance, if the action described in the poem is quick and lively, the poem should also zip along without delay. This can be done by choosing the right words and a fast-moving rhythm.

RUNNING CHEETAH

Running Cheetah like the wind. . . .
Cheetah, running like a bolt of lightning.
Run! Cheetah, Run! Across the field.
Catch your prey before night's end.
Run! Cheetah! Run! Like the wind.

—Melissa Adrouny, grade 4

If the mood of the poem is quiet and soothing, the sound and rhythm of the words should also be slow, as in this lullaby.

Close your eyes, sweet little one,
Go to sleep my dear.
Angels will watch over you,
You need never fear.

Lullaby my baby,
Coo, Coo, Coo-a-roo.
Hush-a-bye my darling,
I love you, love you, love you.

 ## RHYME

A rhyme occurs when two words end with the same sound. This repetition of sounds creates an orderly and pleasant pattern.

Rhyming words can weave a spell,
Or wrap you in a hug,
Might hide you in a secret place
To keep you warm and snug.

Some rhymes pop easily into your head. There are one-syllable or single rhymes, such as bake and cake, cat and hat, or bug and rug.

There are two-syllable or double rhymes, such as ocean and motion, funny and bunny, or double and trouble. There are also three-syllable or triple rhymes, such as conclusion and confusion, created and related, or commotion and promotion.

The most common place to find a rhyme in a poem is at the end of a line.

> Some bears are grumpy
> Some bears are humpy
> Bears are active
> Bears are attractive.
>
> —*Chelsea Kaiser, grade 3*

Dinnertime, 1995, by Desi Lustig.

The snow leopard is a kitty cat,
He has a snowy habitat.

—Tyler Geddes, grade 3

SNOWMAN

In winter it's snowing
The snowflakes are falling.
The wind is blowing
And my mother is calling.

The snowman is built
Out of new fallen snow.
He'll soon start to tilt
When the sun starts to glow.

—Jason Krout, grade 2

Sometimes poets put an inner rhyme in the middle of the lines.

Even my nose knows
Where a rose grows.

If you want to write a rhyming poem, remember it can be hard to find words that rhyme exactly. A rhyming dictionary can help.

This poet uses the names of countries. Although the rhyming words are spelled differently, the sounds are the same.

I will travel around the world.
All the countries I will see.
Maybe Russia, maybe France
Maybe even Italy.
Then when I get back
I'll tell you about Iraq.

—Rebecca Nagle, grade 4

Rhyme that flows naturally adds delight to a poem. A forced rhyme can interrupt the rhythm, mar the mood, or cloud the meaning of the poem.

Here are some examples of forced rhyme.

> A mouse is quicker than a cat.
> It is hard to tell where it is at.

> It is very frightening
> When dogs are fighting.

Occasionally a poet will change the rhythm or rhyme pattern of a poem on purpose to show an unexpected action.

> Blow bubbles, go bubbles,
> Fast and slow, high and low
> Oh, oh, bubble trouble!
> No, no, not that!
>
> SPLAT!

Rhyme Schemes

The way that rhyming lines are arranged in a poem is called the rhyme scheme. The scheme, or pattern, is usually shown with letters of the alphabet. The lines coded with the same letter have the same ending rhyme.

For instance, an *aa* scheme means that two consecutive lines rhyme:

> Never wear a frown   a
> On the way to town.   a

An *aabb* scheme means the first two lines rhyme and the second two lines rhyme:

Never wear a frown	a
On the way to town.	a
A happy smiling face	b
Is welcome any place.	b

You can use as many letters as necessary to represent the different rhymes in a poem. The pattern of the letters shows the rhyme scheme. The rhyme scheme is repeated in each stanza.

CHRYSALIS

How I wish that I could tell	a
What happens in that shiny shell.	a
A striped worm, gold, black and white	b
Sealed himself in tight one night.	b
He hasn't room to shed his clothes	c
But he'll be changed from tail to nose,	c
For when he comes out, by and by	d
He'll be a Monarch butterfly.	d

 REPETITION

By repeating the same word or phrase, you can give your poem a musical quality that connects the parts of it together. You can also use repetition to emphasize important elements of the poem's story and help the reader remember them.

In the story "Snow White and the Seven Dwarfs," the wicked queen asks, "Mirror mirror on the wall, who is fairest of them all?" She asks this question over and over, showing how vain she is.

In the story, "The Little Engine That Could," the engine says, "I think I can, I think I can, I think I can," to help him chug up the hill until he reaches his goal.

A regularly repeated phrase adds an element of delight to a poem. It can give the reader a happy, light-hearted feeling and should be fun to say: "Old MacDonald had a farm, Eee-i, eee-i, O!"

The repeated words in this poem create a flowing rhythm that describes the slow, steady movement of the water:

A PEACEFUL STREAM

A peaceful stream.
A stream flowing flowing flowing;
A stream going going going;
A peaceful stream.

—*Clay McKell, grade 4*

 ## TITLES

The title is a very important part of your poem. It is the first thing the reader sees and should make him or her want to read the rest of the poem.

When you read the title of this poem, "Vice Versa," what do you think the poem might be about?

You probably never thought of this:

VICE VERSA

Do you wonder in the winter
When the leaves are on the ground,
If the trees have turned in somersaults
And flipped themselves around
Until the tops are tucked in tight
Till springtime comes again
And all the raveled roots are reaching
Upward in the rain?

A title can also ask a question and make the reader curious to know the answer:

KATY DID?

Katydid, Katydid,
Katy did, did, did?
What on earth did Katy do?
I don't have a clue,
Do you?

A title can also have a double meaning that is not clear until the end of the poem:

THE GOBBLERS

A turkey gobbles every day
In the sunshine or the rain.
He gobbles as he struts about
Gobbles gravel, gobbles grain.
A turkey gobbles every day
Every day but one,
For once a year, a holiday
Is set aside for fun.
And on that day, it's sad to say,
A turkey's not so perky.
'Cause that's the day,
Thanksgiving Day,
When people gobble turkey.

 ## THE THREE PARTS OF A POEM

All poems have a beginning, a middle, and an end. In the opening lines, you introduce the idea:

If a centipede wore roller skates
And skated down the street,

In the middle, you tell more about the subject or ask a question:

What if he stumbled on a crack
And tangled up his feet?

At the end of your poem, you come to a conclusion. It may be what the reader expects or it could be a surprise:

Turkeys, 1877,
by Claude Monet.

He'd have scrambled legs!

Can you find the beginning, middle, and end of this poem?

> Crocus can't croak; bluebells don't ring
> And birds of paradise don't sing.
> Tulips can't kiss; dogwood don't bark;
> Catkins can't meow nor do larkspur lark.
> Poplars don't pop; willows won't weep,
> But Virginia creepers certainly creep . . .
> And creep . . . and creep . . . and creep!

The first two lines introduce the idea. The next three lines tell more. And the last two lines present the conclusion, with a twist.

 ## EDITING AND REVISING

Editing and revising are tools you should use to judge your poetry and make it better. A poem seldom comes to mind in its perfect form. You will probably change your poem many times before you are satisfied with the results. Even after a poem seems finished, it is a good idea to study it from every angle to see if it needs any final polishing.

Read the words over and over. Say the lines aloud. Does it read smoothly with no rough or awkward spots? Look at the pattern the poem makes on the page. Decide where your work needs to be revised by asking yourself some of these questions:

Is this the best way to say what I have in mind?
Are the word combinations fun to say and nice to listen to?
Are the comparisons fresh and original?
Are the images vivid and colorful?

Do the rhythms repeat a regular beat?
Do the rhymes flow naturally and make sense?
Does the tempo match the mood?
Are the emotions expressed so they will be felt by the reader?
Have I used the best title?
Are the spelling and punctuation correct?

As you find places where you can refine your poem, make any revisions that will improve it.

C H A P T E R   T H R E E

THE FORMS OF A POEM

Poetic forms and formulas
Have different patterns, different plans.
Some are strict and disciplined,
Some, free as gypsy caravans.
Some count words or syllables,
Some depend on rhyming lines,
Some are funny, silly, terse,
Others shaped in word designs.

There are many standard forms of poetry. Some are simple and some are complicated. Some rhyme and some do not. A few of the simpler types are presented in this book. As you become a more experienced poet, you may want to study more complicated forms.

 ## BUILDING BLOCK STANZAS

Lines of poetry are arranged in groups called stanzas. Because more than one stanza is often used to make a poem, stanzas are called poetic "building blocks."

Some lines should stay together
For sound or sense or time.
Such segments are called stanzas
And may, or may not, rhyme.

Some of the most common patterns are the two-line stanza (couplet), the three-line stanza (tercet or triplet), and the four-line stanza (quatrain). These simple forms can stand alone or can be combined to form longer poems.

A couplet is made up of two lines that usually rhyme. They are arranged one under the other and are usually the same length. If the two lines form a complete poem, the poem is called a closed couplet.

An earthquake   a
Is a big shake.   a

Three lines that rhyme in any of several patterns *(aaa, abb, aba, or aab)* make a stanza that is called a tercet.

A worm's a skinny, squirmy shape   a
Without any appendages   b
But lots and lots of bendages.   b

Today the weather   a
Wonders whether   a
Rain and sun can play together.   a

These two lines have a common rhyme in line three.

Butterflies are flitting   a
And grasshoppers are spitting   a
Tobacco juice on the grass.   b

Bees are humming   c
Wasps are thrumming   c
Between the screen and the glass.   b

—Amy Sherman, grade 4

A quatrain is a stanza with four lines in many possible patterns and often rhyming.

He is awake at night,   a
But has a short height . . .   a
The green tree frog is nocturnal   b
And not diurnal.   b

—Nathaniel Everett, grade 3

SCRATCH MY BACK

The two spots which   a
I wish would match,   b
Are where I itch   a
And where you scratch.   b

A quatrain made of two rhyming lines enclosed by two lines with a different rhyme is called envelope verse.

While skating down the street   a
I found a shiny nickel.   b
I bought a juicy pickle   b
And I had a tasty treat.   a

 FREE VERSE

Free verse is an unrhymed form of poetry. The poets who created free verse wanted to break free of traditional rules and patterns and make their own. Walt Whitman and *e.e. cummings* are two of the many famous poets who wrote poems in free verse.

In free verse, the poem's lines can be arranged in many ways. Blank space is often used instead of punctuation to indicate a pause. The lines may be long or short, and made up of words, phrases, or sentences. The poet decides where the lines break.

LOST

I was lost
   and I called home
   from a cafe.
The smell of coffee
   filled the air like a breeze
   of French Roast
   and I shivered.
I saw a worn lady
dressed in rags.
She told me
of her beautiful baby
that she lost
to the Black Plague,
or the "kidnapper"
as she called it.
Her auburn hair glistened
as she talked and I reached
out and touched it.
It felt soft and warm. . . .
There was music blaring
   from a speaker
But to me it only sounded
like a mouse scampering
across the room.

She turned and left.
I saw that my ride was here
and I left but still, still
with questions in my mind.

—*Allegra Wilson, grade 5*

 PATTERN POETRY

One type of free verse is called shaped or pattern poetry. These poems are meant to be seen on paper because of the interesting arrangement of words and lines. The poem itself makes a picture.

A square is a box
A box is a square
Is a box a square
Is a square a box
A box a square is

As John grows ↑   P U
His voice grows ↓
         D
         O
         W
         N

TORNADO POEM

—a—t o r n a d o—t w i s t s

a r o u n d — a n d

a r o u n d — u n t i l

i t —t o u c h e s

d o w n - t o

t h e

G R O U N D

```
        A
       tall
     pointy
    pine tree
   just stands
  there waiting
  to be climbed
       by
       me
```

SNAKESNAKESNAKESNAKESNAKESNAKESNAKE

As you are editing what you've written, be sure to look for ways the poem could be revised to make the pattern a stronger shape. Which of these two diamonds looks better?

A DIAMOND

```
        I am a diamond
 Shining in Daves Avenue School
      a treasure to my family
       A pleasure certainly
    So glittery in the sunshine
          That's me.
```

```
              I
            am a
           diamond
        shining bright
     in Daves Avenue School
   a great treasure to my family
       a pleasure certainly
        so glittery in the
          bright sunshine
             that is
              me
```

—Allison Bonadies, grade 4

LIGHT VERSE AND WORDPLAY

> Your mind might like to play some games
> With witty words and nifty names,
> With homographs and homophones,
> Some homonyms, some palindromes,
> Riddles, jingles, funny puns,
> Epigrams and idioms.

Light verse is lighthearted poetry. It is enjoyed more for the poet's cleverness than for the poem's deep meaning. The thoughts and tricky word combinations are unique and often humorous. Ogden Nash is famous for his playful poetry. There are many types of light verse, including limericks, nonsense verse, and parodies. Much of the poetry in this book is light verse.

Different kinds of wordplay can be used in light verse. Marvin Turban, a poet who is called "the master of wordplay," defines the term as "words playing with each other and with the reader."

The English language is a rich source of words that can be used in different kinds of wordplay. There are more than 600,000 English words, more than in any other language. Because there are only twenty-six letters in the alphabet, which are used to make all those words, some of the words are spelled exactly the same. There are also many words with similar meanings.

Homographs, Homophones, and Homonyms

Homographs are words that are spelled alike but sound different and mean different things: for example, bow (a hair ribbon) and bow (to bend from the waist).

Can you figure out more than one sound and meaning for the following words? Close, lead, read, live, bass, permit, rebel, wind, subject.

Homophones are words that are pronounced the same but differ in spelling and meaning: for example, bear and bare, dear and deer, right and write.

Can you think of homophones for these words? Eight, pair, sense, tea, here, see.

Homonyms are words that are pronounced and spelled the same, but have different meanings: for example, letter (one of the alphabet) and letter (a note); or note (musical note), note (letter), note (to write), or note (to notice). Homophones are sometimes considered homonyms.

Palindromes and Terse Verse

Palindromes are words or phrases that are spelled the same backward as they are forward: for example, mom, dad, sis, did, noon, madam, radar, level, Hannah. Words that spell a new word backward are also palindromes: for example; pot and top, bad and dab, lap and pal.

Figuring out palindrome phrases is a good challenge for quick minds. Check the following to see if they are palindromes:

Neil, an alien.
Dad saw dam, mad was Dad.
Did Sis wow Bob? Wow Sis did!

Terse verse is a short rhyming verse, often made up of only two words, describing a subject. Sometimes the title is even longer than the poem.

PENCIL
school tool
PLANT FOOD
flower power
ALARM CLOCK
morning warning

Riddles, Jingles, and Puns

A riddle is a question puzzle, often with a clever answer.

How does the ocean alphabet begin? A B Sea

What alphabet letter makes a cool summer drink? Iced T

A jingle is a catchy verse that is fun to say and hear. It repeats sounds and rhythms, but doesn't always make sense: Ringy, dingy, zingy, zoo.

A pun is made with words that have the same or similar sounds and different meanings. Usually they are meant to be funny—but are often corny.

He thought he was punny.

Mr. Crow, what do you know
That cawses you to caw?
Is there a cawling cawntest
For laying down the law?

Look for other examples of wordplay in other sections of this book. There are many amusing wordplay books in libraries and bookstores for you to find and enjoy.

Idioms

An idiom is a phrase or a sentence that has a special meaning beyond the meaning of the words themselves. For example, if you say, "He knows the score," you might mean he knows how many points are scored in a game. If you are using the idiom "to know the score," however, you mean that he knows the truth or the real story about something. There are many idioms in our everyday

Gossip, 1991, by Joyce Malerba Goldstein.

speech: out of thin air, batting zero, rocking the boat, running on empty, grasping for straws. Many idioms are part of a dialect or slang language of a particular group or nationality.

 ## RAP POETRY

Rap poetry came from the streets of New York City in the 1970s. Inner-city teenagers were tired of the music they heard on the radio and wanted something different. They began to create poetry about their own day-to-day experiences.

Rap comes from the ancient African tradition of rhymed storytelling. It is set to the rhythmical beat of a drum and is full of energy. In rap poetry, the rhythm is strong and the tempo is fast. Often, the words tell of the hardships and dangers young people face and how they feel about them.

Just for fun, try turning a favorite story into a lively rap poem. This is one of Aesop's fables, told in a new way:

THE FOX AND THE CROW

Out in the woods where I sometimes go
Lived a smart red fox and a dumb black crow.

The crow perched high in a maple tree
Saying "Caw, caw, caw," thinkin' me, me, me!

He held in his beak a chunk of cheese.
The fox was hungry, said "Gimme some, please."

The crow said, "NO!" but the fox was sly.
He looked at me and he winked his eye.

"I love your voice, won't you sing for me?"
The fox begged the crow in the maple tree.

The crow was flattered, so he sang "Caw, caw!"
And the cheese dropped out of his open jaw.

The fox was waitin' with a droolin' mouth.
He grabbed the cheese and he headed south.

This story has a moral for me and you,
Don't listen to a flatter when it isn't true.

SYLLABLE POEMS

A syllable seems like a bend in a word.
Where the tiniest hint of a pause can be heard,
When the tongue takes a turn from an "E" to an "I,"
From an "A" to an "O," a "U" or a "Y."

Words in a dictionary are divided into syllables. There is one vowel sound (a,e,i,o,u) per syllable.

There are nine syllables in these six words. Listen for them as you say the words aloud: "Hip-pet-y hop to the bar-ber shop."

Count how many syllables there are in "Peter Piper picked a peck of prickly pickled peppers."

Some poetic forms have a specific number of syllables arranged in a certain pattern. It is fun to challenge yourself by writing a poem in one of these forms.

Haiku

A haiku is a small poem with a big theme. It contains the seed of an idea that you can continue to think about.

Haiku is a Japanese form of poetry with seventeen syllables composed as an unrhymed, three-line poem about nature.

The lines are arranged like this:

Line 1	five syllables	Loud crashing thunder,
Line 2	seven syllables	Pouring rain and shining sun,
Line 3	five syllables	The rainbow appears.

Although the haiku pattern is mistakenly used for poems about other subjects, a true haiku is about nature. At least one word must identify a specific season—spring, summer, fall, or winter—either by naming the season or including something typical of that time of year. A haiku captures a small scene of something that is happening now. The present tense is always used.

> Trees sway in the wind
> Slowly the leaves start to drop
> Fall has now begun.

—Leah Fredkin, grade 4

Quinzaine

A quinzaine, a French word meaning fifteen, is an unrhymed three-line poem that contains fifteen syllables. The first line makes a statement, and lines two and three ask a question about the subject.
    The lines are arranged like this:

Line 1	seven syllables	Make a statement
Line 2	five syllables	Ask a question
Line 3	three syllables	

> The loud thunder is crashing.
> Are the gods above
> Bowling balls?

> Teardrops hang from the willow.
> Is it weeping for
> My sorrow?

Cinquain

A cinquain is a simple five-line poem that follows this pattern:

Line 1	2 syllables	subject
Line 2	4 syllables	describe the subject

· 42 ·

Line 3   6 syllables   action involving the subject
Line 4   8 syllables   a feeling about the subject
Line 5   2 syllables   another name for the subject

Father
Funny, handsome
Throwing, catching, batting
Teaching me how to play baseball
Daddy

The poem above describes a simple activity shared by a father and child. A true cinquain, however, tries to express a deeper thought or image.

My dad,
With laughing eyes,
Throws the ball at my bat
Cheering when I hit it hard.
Daddy!

Diamanté

A five-line diamanté, named for the French word for diamond, is written in a diamond shape, so the length of each line is important. Diamanté poems seem like pattern poetry because of their shape, but a diamanté has very specific rules, which a pattern poem does not have.

In a diamanté poem, the number of syllables in each line is not important; the number of words in each line is.

There are several variations of this pattern, including the one on the following page; which is very similar to a cinquain:

Line 1	is short
Line 2	is longer
Line 3	is longer than that
Line 4	is longest of all
Line 5	is short

In a diamanté, the types of words are arranged like this:

1 noun	name or subject	Donna
2 adjectives	describe subject	creative, energetic
3 verbs	show action	writes, races, performs
4 adjectives	show feelings	happy, productive, healthy
1 noun	name	Donna

With a little emotion and imagination, you can expand the meaning of the poem and still keep the form basically the same.

Donna
blazing meteor
streaking across the sky
spilling sparks to brighten the night
Donna

Another form of the diamanté has seven lines. It is often written about two different subjects and compares them by moving from the first subject to the second.

Line 1	1 noun	subject #1
Line 2	2 adjectives	describe #1
Line 3	3 "ing" words	related to subject #1
Line 4	4 nouns	2 related to #1, 2 related to #2
Line 5	3 "ing" words	related to subject #2
Line 6	2 adjectives	describe #2
Line 7	1 noun	subject #2

Cat
Fast, greedy
Running, sleeping, hiding
Feline, mammal, animal, rodent
Squeaking, scurrying, sharing,
Small, fuzzy
Mouse

—Kari McClelland, grade 4

Try to write a diamanté of your own. You could compare the beach and the mountains, a dog and a cat, a friend and an enemy, winter and summer.

CHAPTER FOUR

FIGURES OF SPEECH

Poetic devices, called figures of speech,
Are used to define, to describe, and to reach
Beyond the conventional, over the norm,
Way past the average of feelings and form.

Figures of speech are special language tools used by poets and other writers to make their writing more colorful. The various figures of speech can add drama, detail, and depth to poetry.

Some commonly used figures of speech are: alliteration, assonance, consonance, onomatopoeia, simile, metaphor, imagery, hyperbole, and personification.

 ## ALLITERATION

The repetition of beginning consonant sounds in two or more words or syllables is called alliteration: setting sun, barley buns, tiny tot.

A flock flies south with winking wings shining silver in the sun.

To say the same sounds again and again
Like Who, Where, or What and Why, Which or When,
Can tangle the tongue or tickle the ear.
A sound that's repeated is pleasant to hear.

Words don't necessarily have to begin with the same letter to sound alike. Carrot and cereal both begin with "C," but the sound is not the same. Kitty and carrot, pheasant and fish, new, knew, and gnu are alliterative because even though they start with different letters they repeat the same sound.

The repeating sound may also be created with a combination of letters, like "tr" and "wh," as in these poems:

> A tree and a katydid
> tremble together.
>
> *—Daniel Jay Schneider, grade 4*

> The field winds blow from a whisper to a whistle.
>
> *—Meredith Bell, grade 3*

 ## ASSONANCE AND CONSONANCE

Assonance is the repetition of a vowel sound in two or more words or syllables: door and four; feed and read; can and pan.

> Lou's two new cows do choose to use
> A "Moo moo" mood to view Hugh's ewes.

In the last example, did you notice that only two words ("a" and "cow") do not contain the "oo" sound? How many different vowel combinations are used to make the same sound?

Consonance is the repetition of a consonant sound in two or more words or syllables:

> When flitting flies flutter fast
> Toad flicks a lick as they fly past.

Assonance and consonance can also be combined in a poem:

> Pelicans with scooping skills
> Dive for fish to fill their bills.

Brown Pelican, 1835,
by John James Audubon.

Rice ice splashes up from the speeding blades.

—*Justin Kane, grade 4*

ONOMATOPOEIA

Onomatopoeia uses words that imitate the sounds they describe. Buzz, for example, sounds very much like the noise a bee makes. Many animal sounds are examples of onomatopoeia.

> Some words sound the same as the thing
> They are describing, like slam, bang, and zing
> Snap! crackle! pop! ding, tinkle, ring.
> Fizz, sizzle, buzz, crash, clatter, ping!

What do these words remind you of? Quack, grrrr, baa, rat-a-tat, tick-tock, slosh, varoom.

TRAFFIC PATROL

Tweet! goes the whistle
Better stop and walk
Get to your position
BEFORE eight o'clock . . .

—*Kristina Wegscheider, grade 4*

PITTER PATTER, DRIP DROP

. . . I love to watch the silvery drops fall to
         puddles . . .
There comes a chill down my back!
         Pitter-patter
              Drip-drop.

—*Libby Wilhelm, grade 4*

NATURE'S SPARK

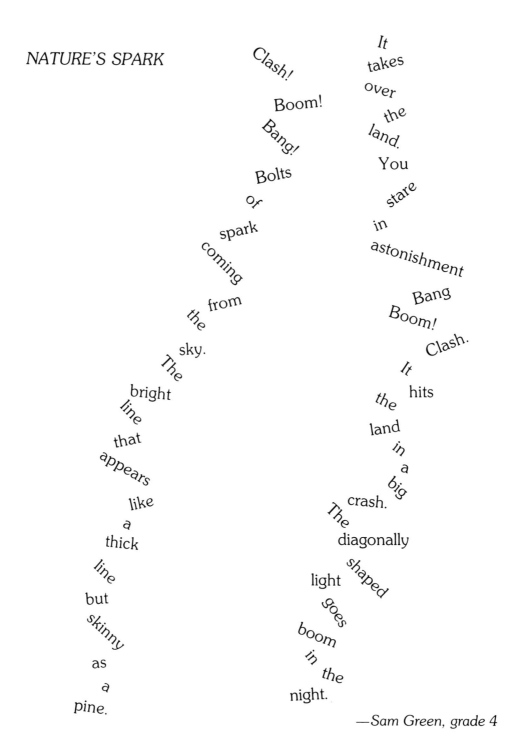

Clash!
Boom!
Bang!
Bolts
of
spark
coming
from
the
sky.
The
bright
line
that
appears
like
a
thick
line
but
skinny
as
a
pine.

It
takes
over
the
land.
You
stare
in
astonishment
Bang
Boom!
Clash.
It
hits
the
land
in
a
big
crash.
The
diagonally
shaped
light
goes
boom
in
the
night.

—Sam Green, grade 4

SIMILE AND METAPHOR

A poet uses similes and metaphors to describe two different things
in a way that makes them seem equal or similar.

> It's nice to compare two similar things
> Saying, "Waves are like hills," and "Kites are like wings."
> Or you may want to state, "The moon is a plate,"
> "The sky is a bowl," "A book is a door
> That opens to rooms you might like to explore."

A simile compares two things by using the words "as," "like," "as
if," "seems," and "appears."

> My legs feel like frozen fish sticks.
>
> —*Marisa Phan, grade 5*

> The mane is like a silver sash, glimmering
> in the pale moonlight.
>
> —*Anthony Frangadakis, grade 4*

Cows in Moonlight, 1992, by Flavia Bacarella.

Its roaring hoofs clapped like thunder on the ground.
The ground shook like the earth's heartbeat.

—*Justin Kane, grade 4*

Skin like fresh falling snow.

—*Han Nguyen, grade 8*

A metaphor compares two things by stating or implying that one thing actually is the other.

The sun is a golden ball rolling around in a sky blue bowl.
A jet is a speeding bullet leaving a trail of smoke behind.

This poet describes how blowing sleet feels:

My face is being stung by bees.

—*Marisa Phan, grade 5*

Another refers to storm clouds as:

Large, black, sulking puffs.

—*Stacey L. Thomas, grade 4*

When creating similes and metaphors, use your senses to compare how the things you are describing look, sound, feel, smell, or taste—and to discover in what ways they are the same.

Can you identify the similes and metaphors in the following poem?

GREY WOLF

A wolf's howl echoes through the forest like a haunting ghost.
His head is tilted towards a pale face of the moon.

His eyes like cold stars, he hunts stealthily.
His fur is made of silk.
Spotting a rabbit his firm, muscular body leaps into action.

Triumphantly, he carries his prize back to his den.
His ears peaked like a mountain, he listens.
Tail swaying like a tree branch, he runs.
Nose made of satin, he smells.

His paws are as delicate as an artist's stroke;
With them he fights
His teeth are like porcupine quills,
Sharp and deadly.

Quietly as a butterfly he returns to his rock below the moon.
With his claws like cold steel, he tilts his head towards the moon.
Once again, he howls.

—Eliana Saffouri, grade 4

 ## HYPERBOLE

Hyperbole is a way of describing something by exaggerating.

Hyperbole overstates the truth to make it more colorful and forceful and to express strong feeling. Use hyperbole! Imagination plays a big part in hyperbole. The exaggeration goes beyond the natural or the real and is so obvious that you know it can't be true. Find the exaggerations in these statements:

Everyone in the world likes ice cream.
The lion had a roar that would flatten all the trees in the jungle.
I felt so low that I could crawl under the belly of a worm.

When hyperbole is used in poetry, it can have a dramatic effect:

Flapping its wings fiercely
An eagle conquered the sky.

—*Trang Ngo*

 ## PERSONIFICATION

Personification gives human characteristics to nonhuman things.

Maples blush so red in fall
'Cause soon they'll have
No clothes at all!

The tree clawed at John with its bony fingers.

The friendly eye of the streetlight
watched over me until I was safe inside.

THE SUN

As the sun
comes out, she
glows upon us.
I try to find
somewhere cool,
    but
     always
      see
       her
       right
        behind
       me.

Sundown, 1894, by George Inness.

She loves herself
and when she's bored
She'll paint
    the sky
        and call
            it
              sunset
Before she says good-bye.

—Aileen Montoya, grade 5

This poem contains all of the different figures of speech described in this chapter: alliteration, assonance, consonance, onomatopoeia, simile, metaphor, imagery, hyperbole, personification. Can you find each of them?

RISING TO ITS PEAK

The moon rises slowly to
Its peak in the sky
Shedding light white as snow
Down to earth. The earth is
Covered with a blanket of
Darkness that swallows up
The white beams of light.
A chilling breeze passes through.
The moon, as if held by steady
Hands, lowers until even with the rising sun.
Once again,
Warmth fills the earth
And the sun starts its
Long journey west.

—*Beth Liefer, grade 5*

 IMAGERY

Imagery is the painting of poetic word pictures. These pictures describe everyday things in ways that appeal to all the senses.

So you can see what I see,
Can sense the scent I smell,
Can hear the sounds I'm hearing
Or feel the things I tell. . . .

To create imagery in your poetry, train yourself to see the ordinary things around you in many different and new ways. Challenge yourself to sharpen your senses. Become more aware of every sensation. Imagine what a leaf looks like to a caterpillar. What is an eagle's-eye view of a mountain stream?

It's easy to feel the prick of a thorn. But it takes concentration to feel a snowflake landing on your hair.

You know the color red. But is it really crimson or scarlet? Maroon? Cherry, tomato, or watermelon?

It's simple to identify the scent of a skunk, but is your sense of smell keen enough to detect the odor of a snail?

Can you hear: The whisper of a whisker when your kitten rubs your leg? The shifting of the lifting of the eyebrow of an owl? The crunching of a munching of a gopher underground?

In order to hear these nearly silent sounds, you must tune out your other senses and listen as closely as you can. The same thing is true when you focus on seeing, tasting, smelling, or feeling.

Sharpening your senses takes time and concentration, but is necessary to do if you are going to write good poetry. Learn every detail you can about a subject. You may not want to include all this information, but once you know it you can pick and choose what to include in your poem.

Which senses are used in the following poems?

CHEETAH RUN

Swift as the wind,
Running with grace,
As his slender body
Breaks the wind like an arrow in flight
Pounding the earth with feet that never seem to
    touch the ground,

Eyes looking straight, never moving,
A face of solid stone
Yellow color and black spots blurring with each movement,
Never breaking the rhythm of the run,
Always running with grace.

—Ronald Lumagui, grade 8

THE NIGHT SKY

The lights turn on;
the stars shine bright;
a purple blanket covers the sky
and turns midnight blue.

The moon shines down overhead
as the sun goes down,
and the breeze flows
through your window as you
sleep through the night. . . .

—Hope Graffius, grade 4

. . . .

CHAPTER FIVE

FINDING THE POET INSIDE OF YOU

A poet is hiding inside your head
Wanting to whisper what words should be said
Waiting and hoping you'll tune in your ear
And quietly listen to all you can hear.

Ideas appear in your head all the time, and usually they just pop out of your mouth in ordinary everyday language. But sometimes a thought is so special that you feel you want to write it down. You wish to say it in the best way possible, with the right combination of words. That idea needs to be a poem.

Poetry is a very personal thing. It comes from deep inside you. Find the poet part of you and listen to its voice.

Now you'll weave your word designs
Into poetic patterned lines.
Hurry! hasten! Don't delay.
The time to start is now, today.

Start with the idea that is tickling your brain. Practice writing different forms of poetry—couplets, free verse, haiku, rap poetry, and others. Try many different rhythms, word combinations, and figures of speech. Keep adding to your idea until it feels complete. Read it aloud. Listen to your words waltz and your sounds sing. The types of poems discussed in this chapter are not actual literary forms, rather suggestions for exploring poetry writing, and for having fun.

 ## SONGS OF YOURSELF

Writers should write about what they know best. The perfect subject to begin with is YOU! You are one of a kind. Celebrate the fact that you are unique. The famous poet Walt Whitman wrote a long poem called "Song of Myself" celebrating many of his characteristics and feelings. Your experiences, thoughts, and feelings will make your poetry different from everyone else's.

> YOU are a treasure; you're one of a kind.
> You're different in body, and spirit and mind
> From anyone else who has lived on this earth.
> You've been a rare child since the day of your birth.
> You're novel, original, second to none,
> A unique individual. You're number ONE!
>
> So fly like a flag that is newly unfurled.
> And use your uniqueness to better the world.

Many races and cultures are represented by the eighth-grade students in the Alum Rock School District in San Jose, California. Using the style of Langston Hughes's poem "The Negro," they wrote about their different ethnic origins.

THE FILIPINO

I am a Filipino:
> Tan like the crisp leaf descending
> From the tree. Tan!
> Tan as the sand washing your
> Soul away.

I've been teased by
> My own peers making jokes about my looks
> And my culture—
> People laughing here
> And there.

I've been shattered
> Into pieces because my dreams
> Had been taken away.
> Is it because of my color?

I've been barren
> With no more hope for who I am,
> By the world misjudging me.

I've been hurt
> By my color with no respect
> From others,
> With clouds surrounding the sorrow.

I am a Filipino:
> Tan like the crisp leaf descending
> From the tree. Tan!
> Tan as the sand washing your
> Soul away.

—Barbara Paras, grade 8

Some other poems had short sections that described skin color or other racial features:

> I am Chinese:
> > Tan as a grocery bag.
>
> > —*Giai Tat, grade 8*

> I am Vietnamese:
> > Tan as the beach on the shore,
> > Tan like the native people in my Vietnam.
>
> > —*Quan Pham, grade 8*

> I am a Choctaw:
> > My skin is black.
> > My soul knows no color.
>
> > —*Eric McEwen, grade 8*

> I am an Indian, a Sikh:
> > Pure as the ocean water
> > And quiet as the clouds above.
>
> > —*Harpreet Hothi, grade 8*

> I am a Punjabi:
> > With long hair and turban
> > And scared of no one.
>
> > —*Gursharon Johal, grade 8*

Name Acrostic

Here's another way to put yourself in a poem. Make an acrostic using your name.

An acrostic is a poem in which a word is written vertically, and each letter begins the first word of a new line.

C aring   C oncerned
O riginal   A rtistic
L oving   R adiant
I ntelligent   L ively
N aive   Y outhful

You can make acrostic poems using other words, too.

C ommunicating   C hallenging
O n   O ur
M y   M inds
P C   P ushing
U sing   U s
T he   T o
E- mail   E xcellent
R oute   R esults

The "I" Poem

Here's another way to write a poem that tells about yourself. Start each line of the poem with the word "I" and a verb. The poem can be any length. It can be a rhyming poem or free verse.

Try one and see what happens!

I am . . .   I hate to . . .
I can . . .   I wish . . .
I never . . .   I will . . .
I wear . . .   I love to . . .
I won't . . .   I like . . .

SEA OF LIFE

I like to swim
in life's great sea,
just floating about
the ocean and me.

I swim with the fish
and race with the waves,
And dance with the mermaids
down in their caves.

I like to swim
in life's great sea.
Go grab a dolphin
and come play with me!

—Jenna Wood-Christianson, grade 5

The "I Am Like" Poem

An "I am like" poem compares you to an animal or a thing using simile or metaphor. This is another way you can use to describe yourself in an imaginative and unique way.

I'm like a mouse,
small, shy with strangers.
Big eyes watch for trouble.
Picky with food.
Impatient for shelter.
I work hard babysitting for cats.
I'm like a mouse.

—Piper Fine, grade 4

I am like a raccoon,
Cuddly cute,
Running about.
Outgoing but shy.
Hyper and active.
Dancin' to music whenever I can,
Out in the sun to catch a tan.
Talking a lot but working hard.
Lots of friends, understanding too,
That's me, a raccoon.

—Heather Isaacson, grade 4

I am like a measuring cup who measures
everything out equally. I scoop up all the
badness in the world and sift it so it's good.
Then I make good things with it. People are
happy to have me because I help them with
problems.

—Melissa Adrouny, grade 4

The tea kettle and I steam and boil
We sing
We are warm and comforting
Kind
Though we are different, we are alike.

—Eliana Saffouri, grade 4

PERSONAL PLACES

Write about the places you know, too. Begin with your home. Describe what's in your room, under your bed, in your closet, or in that drawer you've been meaning to clean out.

WHAT'S UNDER MY BED?

I've got underwear under there
I've even got my teddy bear!
If you want to know the truth
That is where I lost my tooth.
And my rubber snake is missing
I think that it's down there hissing.
And way, way, in the back
You will find a hackysack!

—*Zack Gold, grade 3*

I've got a smelly sock
And a broken lock
A special small rock.

—*Joey Defosset, grade 3*

There is a pair of shorts
And a little rock of quartz.

—*Nathaniel Everett, grade 3*

WHAT'S IN MY CLOSET?

In my closet is the mess;
I can't find my best dress.
Barbies, boxes, dresses, books
But there's nothing on the hooks.

—*Sara Thomas, grade 3*

Flying carpets that have died
racing cars that haven't tried.

—*Sam Rudy, grade 3*

My Mom says I should clean it soon,
At least before the last of June.

—Claire Strouss-Tallman, grade 3

YOUR COLORFUL WORLD

The world is filled with rainbows of color. Each of the many hues
could be the inspiration for a poem. Choose one of your favorites.

When I see red
I see a flower bed
I think of afternoon sunsets
A single red rose
And nail polish on my sister's toes.

—Anthony Frangadakis, grade 4

Yellow
sun in the morning
bright as fire
gives the world warmth
Yellow.

—Khoa Ly, grade 8

BROWN THE EVERYTHING COLOR

Cleveland Browns, playing
Brown jackets all warm.
Brown markers the coach draws with
Brown mud, in the parking lot, under the puddles
Brown dirt from which the grass grows.

—Clay McKell, grade 4

Silver
soft, smooth, shiny moon
Oh, how it brings glistening light
as darkness falls to earth!
Silver

—*Jasdeep Jainy, grade 8*

Green is tomatoes waiting to ripen.

—*Meredith Bell, grade 3*

 THE ANIMAL KINGDOM

Animals are always a favorite subject for poems. Write about your
pets or other animals that you like.

THE DEER

I am the deer gentle and free
Come walk through the forest with me
The trees are my guardians
They keep me safe from harm
The sun is like my mother
It keeps me nice and warm
So come with me to where I live
The forest is my home
Come with me
And see where I roam.
I am the deer,
Gentle and free.
Come walk through the forest with me.

—*Sara Prouty, grade 4*

Thicket of Deer at the Stream of Plaisir-Fontaine, 1866, by Gustave Courbet.

EAGLE

Eagle flies higher than the mountains,
    faster than a jet.
It goes up, up high,
Then drops like it is dead.
Swooping down on its prey,
    smiling gleefully.
Looking around with its sharp, keen eyes,
    right at me!

—Virlyn Acidera, grade 7

As my wings help me glide
through the air
I see the red mountains
and the canyons in the
earth's ground, below.
I smell the sweetness of air.
It is very quiet and peaceful,
but at night I can hear the
howls of hungry wolves.

—Daniel Borunda, grade 6

Bewildering Beasts

Another type of animal poem might describe some kind of bewildering beast, a comical creature that combines the features of two or more real animals.

KANGAROOSTER

A kangarooster leaps about;
A kangarooster crows.
She has a furry body and
A beak stuck on her nose.

A kangarooster has a pouch
For incubating eggs,
A multi-colored feather tail
And claws on all four legs.

A kangarooster is a beast
Bewildering to view
She'd be the main attraction
If you found her in a zoo.

A RHINORABBIT

A rhinorabbit
Has a habit
That is strange to see. . . .

Since you're a poet
You must know it
Won't you please tell me?

Can you write a poem about the rhinorabbit to answer this poet's question? Try to write one about a moosemouse or a bewildering beast of your own.

 ## WHAT IF? POEMS

Poets find many ways to inspire the voice inside them. They might start with the simple question, What if?

What if raindrops came in rainbow colors
    or Kool Aid flavors?
What if they jiggled like Jell-O?

What if pumpkins grew on trees
And started swinging in the breeze
When you were sound asleep below?

What if one broke loose and dropped?
And hit your top before it stopped?
You'd be a pumpkin head, you know.

If, if I were a butterfly,
    If, if I were a bee,
If, if I were a ladybug,
    You would never catch me.

—Tony Alves, grade 6

BEETLE

Beetle, crawling on the wall,
How is it that you do not fall?
If I should climb in such a place,
I would fall flat on my face.

"TO" POEMS

In a "to" poem, the poet is writing to the subject of the poem. It could be written to a person, an animal, a place, or an object.

Have you ever seen a mulberry tree smoking? Every spring for two or three days, circular puffs of pollen are released as the blossoms are nudged by playful breezes. This is the kind of natural event that most people don't even notice—but a poet does!

Mulberry Tree, Little Girl, and Goat, 1988, by Su-Li Hung.

MULBERRY TREE

Shame on you,
Mulberry tree,
Puffing out smoke rings
Back behind the garage
Where no one can see.
Don't you know
That smoking
Can be hazardous
To your health?

This poet was interrupted while she was contemplating a tree, which gives the poem a surprising turn at the end.

Oh, my tree, my lovely tree,
You'll soon be frozen, I can see.
Then there will be no fruit pie.
Just a funeral for you, tree.
How sad I'll be, my lovely tree. . . .

Ouch! A bee is stinging me.

—Moriah McClanahan, grade 5

 ## PEN PAL POEMS

A pen pal poem is written by two people. You and a friend send the poem back and forth, like a letter. You write one line. Your friend adds a line that rhymes. The poem grows as the page goes to and fro.

I heard some exciting news today
Tell me more. What did they say?

Jupiter was hit by Mars.
Are planets playing bumper cars?
Cosmic cinders are raining down,
Grab your umbrella and warn the town!
So cover your head and protect your face
When comets collide in outer space.

 ## NEWS STORY POEMS

A newspaper writer always asks the questions Who? What? When? Where? Why? and How? The news story poem answers those questions in any order in a five-line form.

Line 1	Who?	The sixth grade boys
Line 2	Where?	kneeling on the ground
Line 3	When?	at recess
Line 4	What?	are playing marbles
Line 5	Why?	for the championship

The flowered hat my Grandma wears
to church
each Sunday
smells of the lavender-lined-drawer
that holds her treasured memories.

 ## I-WISH-I-WERE POEMS

The I-wish-I-were poem describes someone you would like to be. It uses many of the questions asked in the news story poem:

Line 1	"I wish I were"	I wish I were
Line 2	who	a telephone repair man

Line 3	where	high above the street
Line 4	what	connecting thick black wires
Line 5	why	to make words travel through the air.

Would you like to be an Olympic gymnast? A high-scoring hockey player? An astronaut on a space station? An Arctic explorer? Try writing a poem about the person you would like to be.

 ## CONTRAST POEMS

A contrast poem is a two-part poem that shows different characteristics of a scene or subject. The first half of the poem describes one aspect; the second half describes another. The poem can be free verse or rhyming.

FOURTH OF JULY

In the morning
flags fly overhead
as the band bangs its way
along the parade route
to the picnic ground.

In the afternoon,
lines of ants swarm
over sticky watermelon rinds
carelessly tossed
on the trampled grass.

 ## WINDOW-FRAME POEMS

A window-frame poem describes a view from the poet's window.

The sun untucks itself from a
blanket of cloud
the webbed warm rays
light up the sky like a light bulb
Lighting up a small room on a dark
night.
                              —*Allison Bonadies, grade 4*

WILD PLUM TREE

All of a sudden, I see you there
White as a whisper, fragile as air
Wearing a wisp of gossamer lace,
Peeking at last from your hiding place.

All summer, all autumn, all winter through
You merge with the forest, hidden from view
And wait for that magical moment in spring
When it's time for your turn to make my heart sing.

 SENSORY POEMS

Sometimes it is a good exercise to try to use all of your senses as
you write. What do you see, hear, smell, taste, and feel about that
one certain subject?

MY CLARINET

Feel the fingers pressed against the hard, warm buttons.
See the audience watch you make a melody in the air.
Hear the tunes so smooth and calm.
Smell the awful perfumes that smell like rotten flowers.
Taste the wooden, vibrating reed.
                              —*Piper Fine, grade 4*

Marine, 1866, by Gustave Courbet.

Saunter across the beach and feel my foot sinking into the blazing
hot sands. . . .
the brisk water splashing me . . .
Seaweed wrapped around my legs. The moist breeze in my face
Listen for the wave to come against the sand crashing like thunder.
Hear the chirping seagulls flying across the sky.

—*Heather Isaacson, grade 4*

Snow is

>as white as an Arctic fox
>as cold as ice
>as soft as a kitten
>as icy as a snowy owl.

—*Laurel Hulme, grade 1*

SONGS OF THE SEASONS

The seasons are a universal topic for poets. You may want to write about the weather, the events, or the feelings of a particular time of year.

THE SNEEZIN' SEASON

Winter is the sneezin' season,
Sniffin', snuffin', wheezin' season.
Common Cold's the sneezin' reason
When it's snowin', sleetin', freezin'.

How I wish for spring to come!

Springtime is so warm, so mellow,
Light and bright and pink and yellow.
Blossoms pop out everywhere;
Springtime fragrance fills the air.

Catkins dangle from the trees
And each playful balmy breeze
Tickles all the grassy tassels
Stirring pollen . . . till I sneeze

And sneeze. And sneeze. And SNEEZE

Ah-ah-ah-ah choo!

My cheeks are like ice
Mufflers, mittens, and frozen fingers
I shiver and shake.

—Jenna Milosovich, grade 4

Cold blue Arctic ice
Ginger cookies and candy

—Kai Van De Pitte, grade 4

Winter
can rip your
soul. . . .

—Desmond Hamilton, grade 3

OCCASIONAL VERSE

Occasional verse is any poem of any style, funny or serious, written for a special occasion or public event. It could be a birthday, an anniversary, graduation, or other celebration. You may want to send a poem to congratulate someone on a special achievement, to say thank-you, or to apologize. Or you can make a poetic party invitation.

A special celebration,
A ball, inauguration,
A birth, or graduation
Should live in memory.

You shouldn't need persuasion
To mark a big occasion,
(Like an alien invasion)
By writing poetry.

The poet included this poem with a baby gift:

JOHN ROBERT'S QUILT

This quilt is warm and cozy
Just the very size
To snuggle and to huggle
And to wipe wet, teary eyes.

One side is soft and cuddly,
The other smooth and slick
To heal an ache or "Ow-y"
And to do it quick, quick, quick.

But best of all it's handy
When nappy time is near
To listen to the quiet
When you hold it by your ear.

 HOLIDAY POEMS AND OTHERS

Holiday poems can be considered a type of occasional verse, marking a special event. This is an acrostic holiday poem:

V alentine's day is coming
A nd so is the
L ovely,
E xhilarating, and
N ice Cupid
T hrowing the arrows
I nside chests so people will be
N ice
E specially to people who hate.

—*Melvin Chen, grade 5*

"Est" Poems

To make an "est" poem, write about the funniest, the scariest, the saddest, or happiest thing that has ever happened to you.

> The stickiest taffy I ever saw
> Stuck to my teeth, to my tongue, to my jaw.
> It sealed my lips, yes, zipper tight.
> And stuck me up for the rest of the night.

Sports Poems

Try writing a poem about your favorite sport or player.

> Fresh dirt drifts up your nostrils
>   as you briskly walk
>   onto the infield.
> Crack of the dirty, wet ball
>   on the new bat.
> The ball zips through the air
>   and hits the first baseman's mitt. . . .
> "Out!" the umpire says.

—Cameron Shutts, grade 4

Number Poems

Try this unusual way to structure a poem. Use the digits in an address or telephone number to indicate how many words are found on each line. For example:

237 Harding Avenue

2   My House
3   Small, white, adobe
7   A touch of Mexico in cold Connecticut.

PRESERVING YOUR POETRY

There's a great deal of value in what you've written. Treasure it. Take care of it. Always keep the original poem in a place where you can find it. Make sure it is signed and dated. Give away copies, not the original.

There are many places to keep your poetry: in a file folder, a notebook, a binder, a card file, a manila envelope, a covered box, a photo album, a file cabinet, a briefcase, or on a computer disk. Your poems can be arranged by subject matter, poetic form, or the date when they were written. Decide which storage place suits you best and then always put your work safely where it belongs.

CHAPTER SIX

SHARING POEMS

When you delight in poetry,
Please share a treasured verse with me
So lilting lines that live for you
Will sing a song in my soul too.
Our thoughts will blend, our minds commune,
And tender hearts will beat in tune.

 MEMORIZING POETRY

Memorizing poetry is one of the nicest things you can do for your-self. It fills your mind with wonderful words, pleasant pictures, and challenging thoughts. It sharpens your senses and focuses your feelings.

When you are sad or lonely, you might remember a special line that can comfort you. Whispering a poetic message can bring joy to someone you love.

Sharing a humorous poem with a friend creates a happy feeling for both of you. Keep these things in mind when you choose a poem to memorize. If you like a poem, others probably will, too.

April Shower, 1992, by Su-Li Hung.

Ways to Memorize

As a young child you probably enjoyed hearing a favorite story over and over again. Before long you knew the lines so well that when the reader paused, you could fill in the correct word or phrase. Soon you knew the story by heart. That was your first experience in memorizing.

Bards were ancient singer-poets who taught people about famous heroes and events in history by setting their poem-stories to music. Sometimes singing or chanting a poem can also help you learn to say it from memory.

Start by memorizing one of your own poems. You probably know it by heart already.

Here are three techniques to try:

The One-Line-at-a-Time Method:
1. Read the poem through several times.
2. Say the first line again and again until you have memorized it.
3. Now do the same for lines two, three, and four.
4. When you learn a stanza, repeat it over and over until it is firmly in place in your brain.

The Write-It-Down Method:
1. Write the poem on a piece of paper.
2. Leave a space and write the first line as many times as necessary until you can do it without looking at the original.
3. Do this with each line.
4. Then write the lines in their correct order.

The Fill-in-the-Blanks Method:
1. Write the poem on a blackboard.
2. Read it over and over until you are familiar with it.

3. Erase one key word in each line.
4. From memory, fill in the spaces with the right words.
5. Continue in this way, omitting more words each time, until you know the whole poem.

Now that you've memorized the poem, you are ready to recite it.

 ## RECITING POETRY

In the days before movies, TV, and rock concerts, variety programs were a popular form of entertainment. They were held in schools, churches, and other public places. The programs included singing, dancing, instrumental music, and "readings." The people giving readings recited dramatic or humorous stories and poems. Famous writers were often asked to compose and read special selections and occasional verse to celebrate important events, such as Independence Day or the inauguration of a president. Maya Angelou read the poem she wrote especially for the occasion at President Bill Clinton's inauguration.

As part of their education, grade-school children were once expected to memorize and recite poems in their classrooms. Once they learned these pieces by heart, they could usually remember them for the rest of their lives.

Although the art of reciting poetry is not as popular as it once was, it is still a good way to express yourself, to learn to be comfortable in front of an audience, and to develop public-speaking skills. It's also fun to share what you've written with others.

Poems could be used for special classroom occasions, such as holiday or birthday celebrations, assemblies, and back-to-school or open-house programs for parents. Poems can be written to introduce the months or seasons, new school terms, or study units. Recited poems also make nice additions to musical programs.

The hardest part of reciting poetry in front of others is overcoming the fear of doing it. The best way to get over this "stage fright" is to believe in yourself. When you are determined and prepared, you will succeed.

At first, you might want to practice by yourself. Repeat your poem in your head as you ride your bike, do your chores, or before you fall asleep at night. You could even use a picture, a pet, or a stuffed animal as an audience. But practice, practice, practice.

You might also want to practice saying the poem in front of a mirror so you can see what you look like. The expression on your face should match the mood of your poem.

If you have a tape recorder, you might want to record how you sound when you say the poem out loud. Practice different ways to present the poem.

When you are ready to try to recite the poem before an audience, choose good friends or family members who are not critical. Only after you are sure of yourself will you be able to accept suggestions without being hurt by them.

Here are some more helpful tips that will get you ready to present your poem in public:

- Stand straight and tall with your hands and arms relaxed.

- Before you begin, announce the title of the poem and the name of the poet.

- Avoid sudden or awkward movements while you are speaking. They will detract from what you are saying.

- Make the sound of your voice fit the feeling of the poem. Is the poem exciting? Funny? Or sad?

- Say the words clearly and loudly enough to be heard at the far end of the room where you are speaking.

- Speak slowly so the words make sense.

- Pay attention to punctuation.

- Do not pause just because you come to the end of a line. Finish the sentence or thought.

- Speed up or slow down to suit the mood and tempo of the poem.

- Be sure to make eye contact with the people in the audience.

 ## POETRY PARTIES

A poetry party is another fun way to share your poems. Friends recite poems to each other.

In many cities, such as New York and San Francisco, poetry parties are often held in bookstores. Poets bring their favorite poems to read to one another and to an audience of poetry lovers.

To create a party of your own, you might want to invite family and close friends for an afternoon or evening of poetry. Invite anyone who would like to read a poem to join in.

You could also have a party in your classroom at school. Ask your teacher if you could use the classroom during lunchtime. Invite your teacher, classmates, and others to come and listen. Your classmates can read their own poems or other poems that they like. The more people reading, the better. Limit the number of poems each person will read to give everyone an opportunity. Arrange the chairs to form a circle and let each person stand up to read in turn. Pause for applause after each poem and be sure to thank the audience with a nod or a bow.

Often, there is no discussion of a poem after it is read. Most poets expect their listeners to think about the poems for themselves. But you and your group can decide what you'd prefer to do.

The "Garden Flowers in Color" Book, 1985, by Marion Lerner Levine.

Talk to your class officers, teachers, and principal about arranging a school-wide poetry reading, including students from all grade levels.

To plan a poetry party in your town or city, talk to your local community librarian or a nearby bookstore owner. Invite students from both private and public schools to participate. You can make flyers announcing the event and distribute them through your local library or school.

✿ GIFTS OF POEMS

Poems can be kept to yourself, but they are also wonderful messages to send to others.

Here are a few of the many nice ways you can present your poems to your family and friends:

> written on scented paper
> rolled and tied with a ribbon
> mailed on a picture postcard
> sent flying on a paper airplane
> written with sidewalk chalk
> dangling from the ceiling (like a mobile, hanging on a ribbon)
> spoken on an audio tape
> made into a video
> sent by computer through E-mail

You could also leave your poetry in a special spot to be discovered by the person you are giving it to:

> inside a pocket
> on a mirror
> on the refrigerator door
> in a lunch box
> on the dashboard of the car
> hung on a doorknob
> in a bouquet of flowers
> on the computer screen
> on a self-adhesive note

For fun, turn your poetry into secret messages, treasure hunt clues, songs, jump-rope jingles, cheers, prayers, marching chants, slogans, or sayings printed on a T-shirt.

With sharpened sense you're aware
That poetry is everywhere.
Nights are cozy, days are bright
When you write, recite, delight
In words arranged to dance and sing,
To waltz or rumba, sway or swing.

Make sure your pleasure never ends,
By sharing poems with your friends.
Arrange a party, tuck a note
Inside the pocket of a coat.
A poem is such a nice surprise
To warm the heart and please the eyes.

FURTHER READING

Alexander, Arthur. *The Poet's Eye.* Englewood Cliffs, NJ: Prentice Hall, 1967.

Cosman, Anna. *How to Read and Write Poetry.* New York: Franklin Watts, 1979.

Hopkins, Lee Bennett, ed. *Side by Side: Poems to Read Together.* New York: Simon & Schuster, 1988.

Janeczko, Paul B., ed. *Poetry from A to Z: A Guide for Young Writers.* New York: Macmillan, 1994.

Kemper, Dave; Nathan, Ruth; and Sebranek, Patrick. *Writer's Express: A Handbook for Young Writers, Thinkers, and Learners.* Burlington, WI: Write Source Educational Publishing House, 1994.

Lawitter, Pamela. *Poetry Parade.* Santa Barbara, CA: The Learning Works, 1987.

Livingston, Myra Cohn. *Poem Making.* New York: HarperCollins, 1991.

Prelutsky, Jack, ed. *For Laughing Out Loud: Poems to Tickle Your Funny Bone.* New York: Alfred A. Knopf, 1991.

———. *Read Aloud Rhymes for the Very Young.* New York: Alfred A. Knopf, 1986.

———. *The Random House Book of Poetry for Children.* New York: Random House, 1983.

Rodale, J. I. *The Synonym Finder.* Emmaus, PA: Rodale Press, 1978.

Terban, Marvin. *Eight Ate: Homonyms.* New York: Clarion Books, 1982.

————. *In a Pickle: Idioms.* New York: Clarion Books, 1983.

————. *It Figures: Fun Figures of Speech.* New York: Clarion Books, 1993.

————. *Mad as a Wet Hen: Idioms.* New York: Clarion Books, 1987.

————. *The Dove Dove: Homographs.* New York: Clarion Books, 1988.

————. *Time to Rhyme: A Rhyming Dictionary.* Honesdale, PA: Boyds Mills Press, 1994.

————. *Too Hot to Hoot: Palindromes.* New York: Clarion Books, 1985.

I N D E X